Prinaka

a day sketching in Dhaka

by Rob Fairley

Introduction

In a lifetime there are few moments which, when viewed in retrospect, become very defined turning points ... meeting a partner, someone close dying, happenstance ... I have encountered only three or four. This is the story of one of them.

I left Edinburgh College of Art in 1975 and that summer was offered the chance of directing and co-producing a production of Don Giovanni at a small Festival in tropical Australia. I turned it down and instead chose to spend the following five years living on my own, an hermetic existence, on an island in the Scottish West Highlands. I made ephemeral land art and lived as much as possible off the land.

Eventually I moved to the mainland and took on the tenancy of a croft with no neighbours for many miles. By the final decade of last century my working life had evolved a pleasant rhythm ... I spent the Spring and Autumn climbing in the Himalayas and the sketchbooks filled on these expeditions produced exhibitions in Edinburgh and London that subsidised the next expedition to the Greater Ranges.

Then two things occurred: when en route to the North side of Annaupurna in Nepal, I met a gentleman who seemed to know what the future held for me … a story told in "An Olympus in the Dream", then, in November 1992, when climbing at altitude I became aware that I had lost my sense of balance and that something had changed in my head. I got myself off the mountain and, eventually, back to Kathmandu where a perforated eardrum was diagnosed.

I became increasingly unwell (I vaguely remember my friends Mike Woolridge and Jon Tinker visiting me in my hotel room and leaving me with industrial quantities of antibiotics). Slowly I recovered enough to organise a flight back to the UK. In those far off days the cheapest option was to backtrack to Dhaka in Bangladesh. This involved small (ish) feeder flights between Nepal and Bangladesh then an international flight from Dhaka to Heathrow. The cheapest way to do it meant a two or three day stopover in Bangladesh and that is what I was forced to do.

Rob Fairley in 1992 by Mal Duff

Maybe because I have always lived and worked in fairly isolated places one of my great pleasures is exploring (getting lost in) cities which are new to me. The process is not complicated and involves a lot of aimless wandering and copious amounts of tea and coffee.

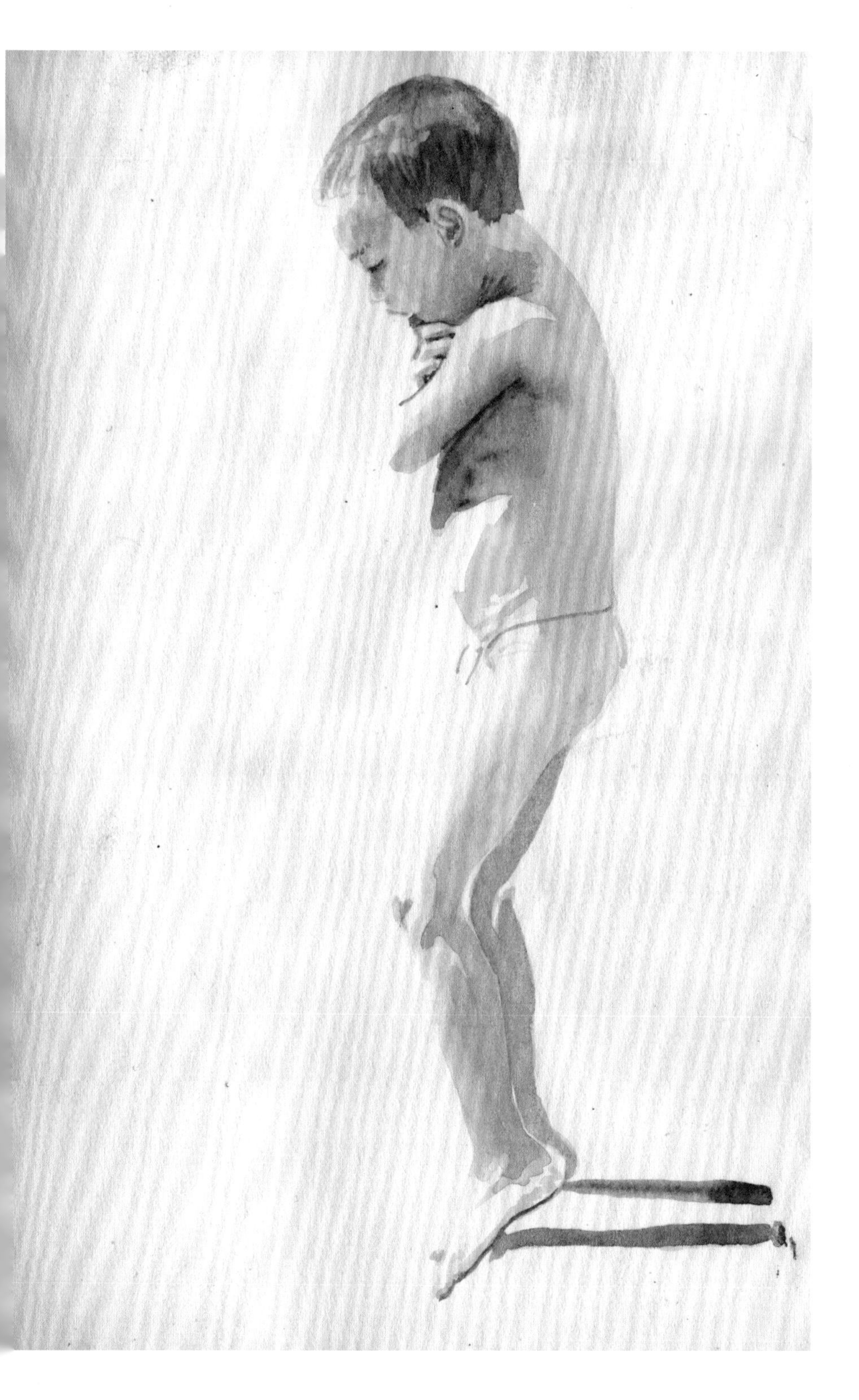

Over the years I have developed many ways of being able to draw while hiding what I am doing thus not gathering an audience however, when drawing the wee boy on the previous page, I was spotted by this gentleman who was selling oranges. Despite a lack of common language, he asked me to draw him. I did two portraits, this in the book, and another on a scrap of paper he produced.

The man who wanted to
have his portrait drawn.

These boys found the orange seller in the previous sketch posing for his portrait very funny; the banter between them, which sadly I could not understand, was obviously extremely amusing and enjoyed by all around.

Street children. boy at
back has stunning thin legs

I started out in the heart of Dhaka's commercial district but had now wandered a long way and was rather disorientated. It was very hot. I sat down in the shade to watch a group of women working on the road at the same time trying to figure out exactly where I was. I bought a glass of tea from a nearby vendor and tried to work out from which group of streets I had emerged ... I began to realise that it was impossible ... and I had no idea where I was.

Woman working a road – breaking stones.

woman breaking stone for road. Strange that this is one of the few women I have seen — small girl on previous page & opposite is her daughter — also breaking stones.

This wee girl is utterly delightful. She adopted me and helped keep curious crowds of kids (and adults!) at bay. Wears pink(ish) shorts – too large for her and thus rolled up at the top. A cord necklace and a yellow band – with hair band which we chose for her from one of the street traders.
Also previous three pages and next eight.
Two drawings given to her.
I first encountered her when she began to follow me around one of the small [illegible] streets. To begin with I paid little attention as I had been followed around all morning. However whilst drawing the first [illegible] several pages

As I sat drawing, (always a good way of putting blind panic on hold) and sipping my tea wondering what my next move should be, I became aware that although there were still many people walking up the street towards me, the flow in the other direction had stopped. I turned round to find out the reason. There stood my guardian angel, though not quite how I had ever imagined her. Small, thin, and wearing little more than a pair of baggy pink shorts several sizes too big for her, she had big soulful eyes full of humour and the most amazing grin. She was standing holding her hands out horizontally stopping all traffic, so that I could see what I was drawing. I laughed and smiled my thanks. She danced over and asked, in halting English, if I was lost "cos people don't come here". I agreed that I was indeed lost, which information she immediately found hilarious and volunteered to "help".
I bought her a glass of tea.

Although I did not realise it then, I was about to embark on the most amazing and fun-filled working "collaboration" I have ever experienced.

which she watched me closely while I scribbled the first sketch - then went up to him and whispered something in his ear. He looked up and posed wonderfully for the second attempt. It is not v. good because I was surprised and felt a little embarrassed. From then on we were definitely a team! She persuaded people to pose - cleared unwanted bodies out of the way - controlled any crowd which inevitably congregated wherever I was trying to draw. On one occasion she held up all the traffic both pedestrian and vehicular while I completed a sketch and took a photograph. If anyone stepped out of line she became most indignant and gave them a piece of her mind. She found me places to get a drink - not easy thing - but once she realised that she would get a coke as well the problem of my thirst was well and truly solved!

Only once was she thwarted when that she watching me of the local snake charmers. He posed for a couple of photographs but when I produced this sketch book my activities became a serious counter attraction and despite the wee lassie's protestations we were sent on our way. — The two of us sneaking off down a side street giggling and grinning at each other while the charmer yelled after us and waved a large grey snake in our direction. She found it v.v. amusing — and led me to the most obscure coke stop!

Very strange how a close relationship can develop between two people thirty years or so difference in age and no common language.

While photographing two men painting a coke advert hoarding — I managed one shot then the wee lassie started leaping around and shouting to get them to turn round — I then had to photograph them again!

I am still not sure whether she was following me or leading me!

She asked my name and told me her parents had named her Prinaka but many of her friends called her 'Ovia' (which I have since learnt means "painting" in Bengali) because her "favourite bit of the world" was to sit and draw. She was fascinated to see that I drew with a brush not a pencil and giggled with delight to realise that my tea was also the water for the watercolour paint.

The drawing on the left of the previous page is me showing her how I "draw" and with her trying to pose and look at the paper at the same time. The sketch on the left hand page here involved her "posing" and me drawing, in tea water, and then her adding the colour. It all had to be done with extreme speed as the heat dried the tea on the paper very speedily.

I think this is the only time any model has posed, and painted, for me! It was wondrous fun. I had no Bengali but she had rudimentary English and we shared poor Hindi ... it seemed we had become a team.

Teams require a leader and it very quickly became obvious that in this team that position was not going to be filled by me!

She suddenly looked very serious and obviously thinking hard said "Rob now I must work for my father, you stay and I come for you after 2 hours. Tum mere saath aao?" I obviously looked puzzled for she grinned and after a moment's thought said "No good Hindi I think. You come?" adding with a grin, "I find people you draw."

I apologised for the fact that my Hindi was so very poor and that I was sure hers was better adding that I would love to go with her if I would not be embarrassing or in the way. She giggled and jigged with delight. "OK you come. First one more drink?" indicating to the tea vendor with an almost dismissive wave of her hand that two more glasses of tea were required.

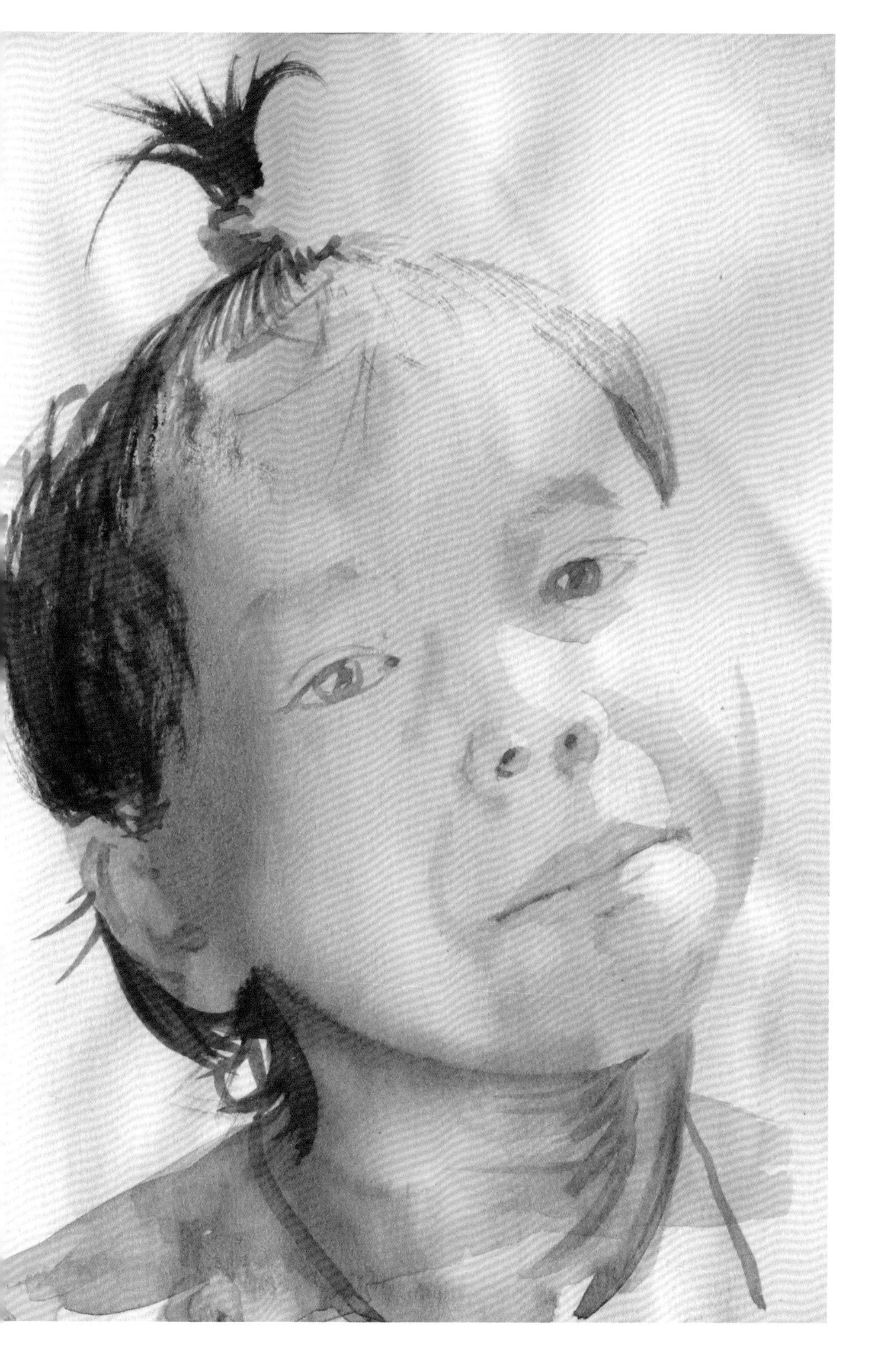

We sat sipping our tea and I asked her what she was helping her father with. "My father is making this" she answered, digging in the folded over part of her baggy pink shorts and producing a small polythene bag holding a couple of dozen or so tiny metal tubes each with a ring attached to the top. "What are they?" I asked. "Tabeez" she said, "like stone you wear in your neck". Back in those long distant days I wore, on a piece of string, a piece of turquoise obtained years before on the Nepali/Tibetan border. "What are tabeez for?" I asked... and with much giggling and demonstrating the full extent of our lack of joint language ... the tea seller being coerced into translating or simplifying concepts from Bengali to Hindi and back to Bengali again before Prinaka translated to something I could understand. She explained that they were amulets worn on the arm or round the neck and which could hold charms or prayers. "My father make, I sell."

"Come, we go now, I work then take you home," she announced. "You pay tea. Bring drawing book." I did what I was told and followed her into a labyrinth of close knit streets and alleyways.

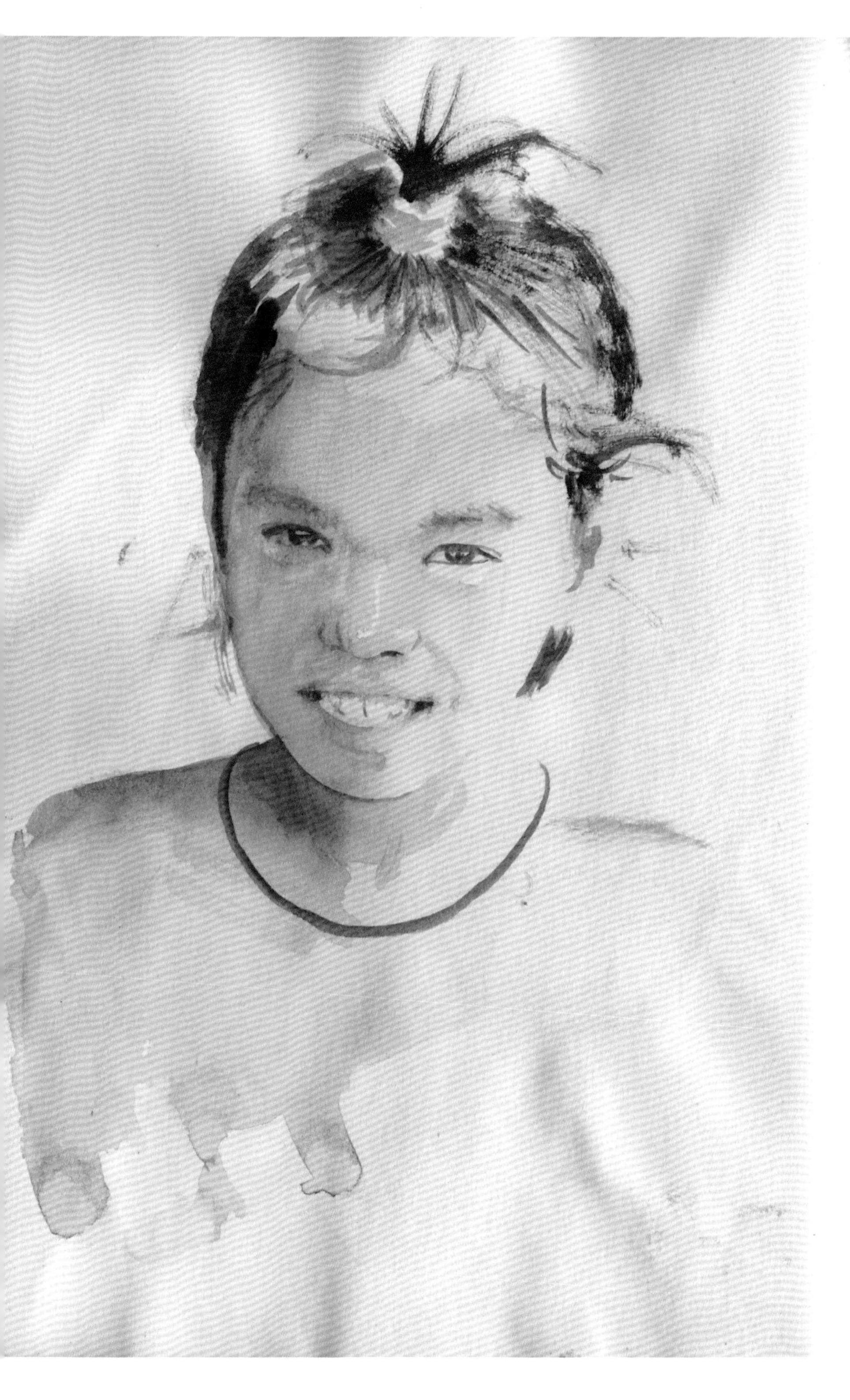

I had no idea what I had let myself in for but somehow trusted my young guide. We walked briskly through the crowds and though there were several things I wanted to stop and draw, or look at, or enquire about ... it obviously was not an option. Suddenly Prinaka stopped and pointed to a young lad sitting on a kerb, his head in deep shade but the rest of him open to the glaring heat and sun, he was mending and cleaning shoes. "Rob, I sell to him and get money ... you draw him." She skipped away and produced her bag of 'tabeez' ... a deal was obviously made for the lad produced a taka note and a few coins ... a few "tabeez" were handed over ... she then whispered in his ear and he briefly glanced round at me then back at her. She took his head in her hands and pointed it in my direction and very obviously issued a command not to move as he didn't until I waved that I had this sketch. She skipped through the crowds and looked over my shoulder, "It OK drawing ... we show him". We showed the lad and inevitably a crowd began to gather to see what was going on. Prinaka however was in business mode and shooing the crowd away insisted that we move on. She thanked her friend/business partner/dealer and we were once again on our way.

The noise and heat in these enclosed spaces was extraordinary and probably because of still being deaf in one ear I found my sense of balance quite odd ... since breakfast I had only had the two teas when I first met Prinaka so I was also probably quite dehydrated. After about 20 minutes we passed (at brisk speed) a shop selling bottles of Coca Cola and I touched her shoulder and suggested we go back and stop for a drink. She looked shocked. "Rob, VERY expensive" she said. I assured her that I would buy and that I needed to stop because I was not very well. I bought two bottles of coke and we sat down on the pavement. She swigged a gulp and choked and giggled and then took another sip. "Rob, I never have. It's nice. Thank you."

"You sick?" she asked. I said I was OK and tried to explain the problem but describing high altitude mountaineering to a lassie who had only ever known the sweltering hot, flat streets of Dhaka proved to be beyond our linguistic abilities. She smiled, held up a hand to stop me, laughed and said "Anyway it's OK today I look after you."

She leafed through the sketchbook and suddenly looked up "Rob you did two of ____ "(she mentioned the name of the shoe maker but I have no record of it). "This more better ... he look happy ... I should've showed him it ... next time show me all OK." From my point of view the sketch done without the model being commanded not to move was obviously freer and a better likeness ... but it was interesting that young Prinaka agreed. We finished our drinks and went back to work.

We made a couple of other deliveries of tabeez and I began to realise that she had a network of dealers who bought wholesale from her and sold them on. "Prinaka, if I bought a tabeez from you how much would it be?" I asked. "It's OK I give you" she grinned in answer. "Yeah but maybe I want to buy ... how much do you sell them for?"
She thought for a moment or two and then said "Rob, we close to my friend's father's shop ... can you draw her and I maybe give as present ... then I give you tabeez OK?"
With my investigation into the economics of tabeez trading effectively deflected I agreed to the deal.
"Rob, it will not be easy to draw my friend."
"Why?"
"Cos she is ... how you say? Not like people?"
"Shy?"
"Yes, very very shy ... this is the shop."
Squeezed between two decaying concrete buildings was a corrugated iron shack which at some point in the past had been painted blue, with a wooden shelf projecting into the street. I was introduced to the owner who sold cigarettes, sweets, the odd vegetable plus various other odds and ends that I did not recognise, though by the exchange of a few taka for two or three tabeez he was obviously also part of her dealership. Prinaka then very obviously asked where her friend was and by the constant glances at me introduced him to the plan. I was handed a sheet of paper and told to stand in the shadows then Prinaka went into the centre of the street and called. Eventually a head appeared from a window and Prinaka made a mistake cos she turned and grinned at me effectively giving the game away!

The sketches here were made, along with the commissioned version, as the two girls chattered (shouted) away at each other, Prinaka immovable from the centre of the 'street' (in fact no more than an alleyway) and her friend quite determined to stay undercover. The shopkeeper and I found it all very funny. The commission was accomplished, and my model and her Dad liked the sketch which my dealer presented them with. Immediately we were on the move again, the dealer skipping ahead and encouraging me to keep up!

This lassie was v. shy but her
curiosity at what I was doing
kept prompting her to peer from
behind a shop. The resulting
drawing created much hilarity in the
street and caused a large audience to gather – this
of course made my model even more shy – she eventually
disappeared!

Prinaka's "dealership" was extensive and every ten minutes or so we stopped to collect money and hand over new stock. It was, however, painfully obvious that the sums being exchanged were very small, rarely more than 2 taka (back then the exchange rate was around 40 taka to the dollar) and very often the money handed over was only very small value coins. Everyone, however, had made some sales and the boss seemed happy with the way her day was going.

"You have food Rob? What do you call it? Lunch? ... I take you good place ..."

"OK Prinaka but I pay OK?"

"Maybe no money ... he a friend."

Eventually we came to an elderly gentleman who was selling bananas, chillies, garlic, onions, potatoes and various other vegetables. He was also cooking a delicious smelling concoction in a large pot over an open fire and had various open breads warming on a grill.

"Sit Rob ... I get" I sat in the shade on the pavement while she went to speak to the chef. Moments later she was back and handed me a fresh bread filled with what appeared to be a banana curry with vegetables and beans. "Eat ... I get for me." It was glorious and unlike anything I have ever had before (or since) contriving to be startlingly spicy and hot and yet sweet all at the same time. "What is it Prinaka?" I asked "Kanchkolar Dom is ..." she pointed to the banana "... and ..." pointing at the vegetable mix ... "we call Shukta ... I like."

"So do I."

We sat and ate in companionable silence for a while and watched the world go by.

Man [illegible] bananas in [illegible].

"Rob?"
She had nipped across to the "chef" and returned with two glasses of tea and handed me one as I finished a sketch of folk passing by.
"Rob? What you do with drawing? You sell? In your country?"
"I do not sell these but I sometimes try and make better copies to sell."
"You have to carry round the street of your country to sell?"
"No ... there are shops called galleries which sell them for me ... they keep some of the money."
"In your country too?" she was suddenly indignant, "My friend's father he good he only take one or two paisa for each tabeez he sell for me but some of them sell for two maybe three or four times what I sell and give me nothing". We commiserated with each other over the unfairness of the art world.
"Will you make 'better copy' of me to sell?"
This was of course the question I really did not want to be asked!
"Oh Prinaka ... I would love to try and paint you properly ... IF I could ... and you would be VERY difficult ... If I could I would want to keep it to remember you ... I would not want to sell."
My young dealer was wondrously pragmatic ... "Of course you sell, you always must sell, you not sell then your family die ... your daughter she take your drawings in the streets in your country?"
"Sadly I have no children Prinaka."
"Ah so that why you have to use shop ... if you had daughter then she would sell and it would be OK ... I sell your drawing here ... maybe 5 taka or 10 taka ... good ones ... like of me ... much more."

Her eyes were gleaming with entrepreneurial delight. "Come Rob I much work today yet ... we go."
I went to pay the chef but she grabbed my arm "NO no ... no money ... he tell me that you sitting eating means many stop to watch and buy from him. He has sold very much many more what he expect ... he promise it free tomorrow ... if we come back. He VERY happy. It is good."
We walked on .... back to work .... my brain doing triple ethical somersaults and coming to no satisfactory answer.
(Back home I did try two 'proper portraits' of Prinaka ... one watercolour was owned by my father in law and after his death by a close friend ... the other ... an oil ... was I think destroyed ... maybe this is the start of the definitive one?)

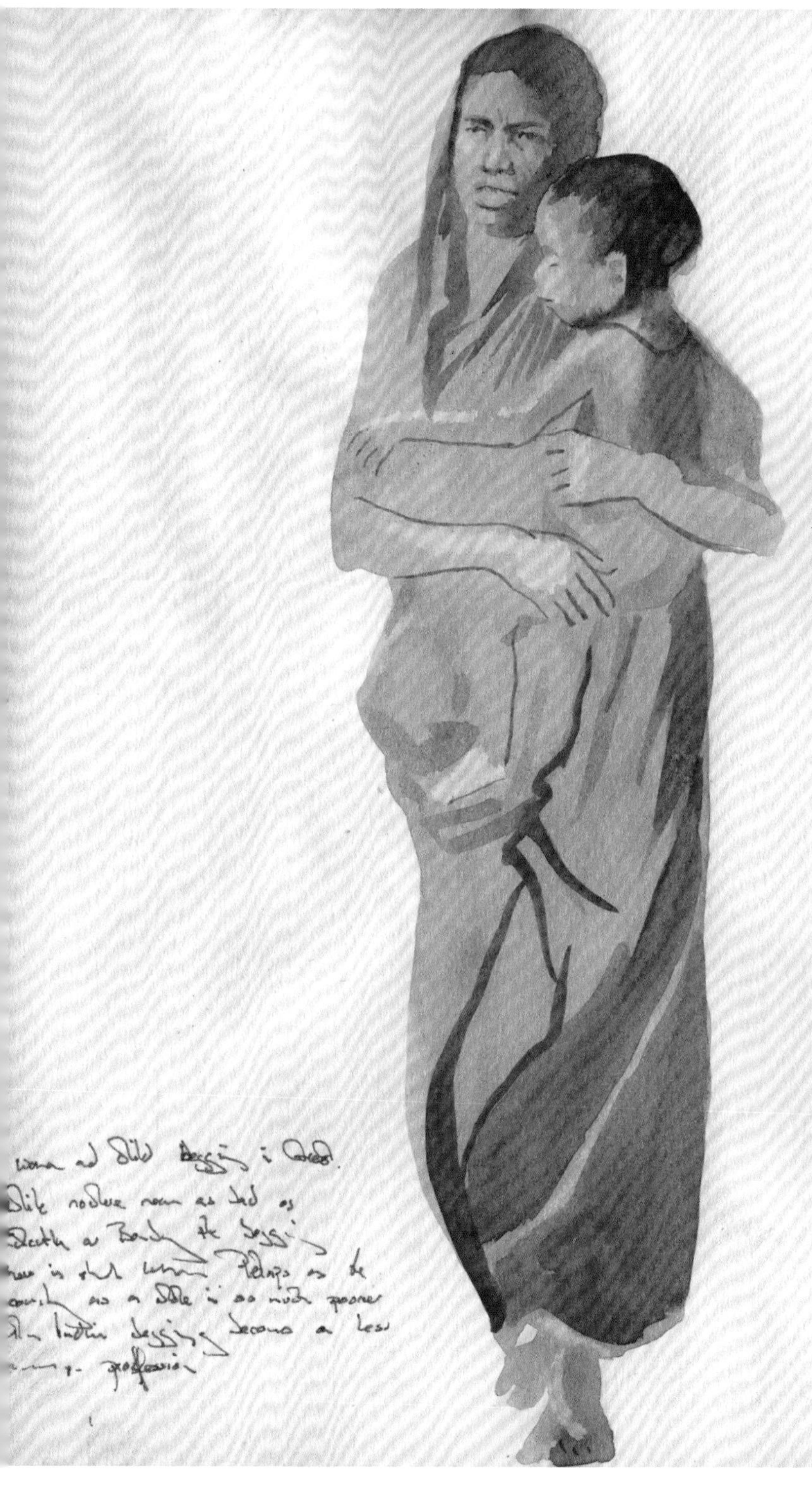
Woman and Child begging in
Child nowhere near as bad as
in Bombay the begging
Perhaps as the
country as a whole is so much poorer
begging becomes a less
profession

Slowly I began to realise that there was a defined pattern to Prinaka's dealership. The majority were street shoe repairers (and polishers), like the lad in this sketch, or were stalls selling tobacco or paan ... all were male owned or certainly male run.
"Prinaka, do you do this every day?"
"I do once / twice a week, two days I get my father's materials for him".
Actually the word or term 'materials' took about twenty minutes to translate so that we were sure we understood each other ... much good humour, a lot of laughter and, for once, my innate inability to try and speak another language was in abeyance ...
"Rob you Bengali get really good" .... she giggled after one of my attempts ... and then collapsed into the gutter in a paroxysm of laughter ... gasping "I good teacher" ... as she struggled, still chuckling, to her feet.
"One day I try go school."
"You want to go to school?"
"NO ... I go to school ... but only one day... I like school ... I learn read and write and English, counting, geography ... my father also teach me English after work ... I need help him work so school one day only."
"The boys you sell tabeez to ... do they go to school?"
"No. Most no parent. My father says school important."
"If your father did not tell you to go then you would not go?"
She paused for a moment. "If I did not discover how fun ... then maybe. But it good, I like."

A couple of years earlier I had come across an exhibition of Bangladeshi rickshaw art in the British Museum in London ... They were startling, colourful, brilliantly executed images and I was quite anxious to see some for real. The alleys we had been traversing for most of the time were too narrow for rickshaws though we had squeezed past the odd one. I explained to Prinaka what I wanted.
"OK Rob, it easy. I have one shop for tabeez ... we cross big road, I find you rickshaw to draw."
Sure enough we shortly exited onto a main thoroughfare "I find you good one with nice driver, stay here." She vanished into the maelstrom of traffic and people to reappear some minutes later with a piratical looking young man dressed in a very bright shirt and with a rickshaw in tow. "He show you and happy for us to paint him."
"Ask him how much Prinaka."
"We pay him?"
"I pay him yes ... because I am taking away his work ... he could have a customer while I paint him so I pay the fare."
A deal was made and for a few taka a "sitting" was arranged. I dug in my bag for a bigger sketch book and coloured paints. "Rob, you never show me this," she said obviously disappointed that I had kept something from her. Strangely I felt guilty. I apologised and agreed she could look through it later.
We attracted a considerable crowd which eventually brought us to the attention of a passing policeman. He elbowed his way to the front of the crowd and asked me what I thought I was doing.
"Painting," I replied.
"Why do you come here?"
"Because I like it."
"What is it you like? You do not like this?" He was quite aggressive in his challenge and gestured at the rapidly thinning crowd and glared at Prinaka who was standing protectively firm, but for once saying nothing.
"I like it very much," I replied

"You a tourist?"
"Yes", I said, "I suppose you could call me a tourist".
"You can't be", He stated firmly, "Here we not get tourist".
With this firm statement of fact he strode off. The rickshaw driver grinned at me and shrugging his shoulders said something to Prinaka who grinned at him. The crowd rematerialised from nowhere and with a great sense of solidarity we completed the sketch; the only time in my life that, as I completed a drawing, and closed the book, I received a round of applause.
Prinaka seemed delighted that her prodigy had performed to her satisfaction and it seemed that not showing her the A4 coloured sketchbook had been forgotten.

We were now in a much more affluent part of the city and my young guardian asked if I would mind if she left me for a few moments while she went to see various traders who were working on the street.
"If you with me, big crowd. More quick just me. Do not move Rob."
She vanished and I took stock of my position. If I was lost when she 'found' me I was most certainly utterly lost now. Because of the sun I had a rough idea in which direction my hotel lay but only very approximately. I made myself as invisible as a six foot westerner could in this part of the city and made drawings of some of the people.

It was very different from the areas we had been walking through for most of the day, Western almost. I sat drawing two women shopping, who could have come from any multicultural high street anywhere in the world, but for the shopping bags, and mused over the day. I had left the hotel curious about Dhaka certainly but also with the very deep and real concern that my career, both as a mountaineer and as an artist, might be over. All my work from school days on had been to do with wilderness, solitude and high mountains. If my perforated eardrum was going to be a constant problem, that might all have to change. A few hours later, thanks in no small part to a tiny, intelligent and constantly amusing wee girl, I realised that not only could I work in one of the flattest, lowest lying and deeply inhabited cities in the world but that I enjoyed it.

Three smartly dressed children stopped to see what I was doing. Though obviously curious they were not brave enough to come across and look at what I was drawing. The girl with the headscarf was wearing an immaculate cornflower blue suit and her scarf could have been semi transparent white silk ... there was not a mark on it. She was wearing smart flip flops.

"Drawing OK ... is good. Why you draw them?"

The voice from behind startled me, though it took micro-seconds for me to recognise it. How long had she been there I wondered. Was she the reason the others had not come to look at what I was drawing? I looked round and grinned at her.

"I draw them because I wait for you."

"Now you not never want draw me."

I looked at her in bewilderment.

"Prinaka, of course I want to draw you, you are a friend. A very clever and very pretty friend."

"I cannot wear ... like that ..." she stared over my shoulder at the other three and for the first time in the day seemed upset and close to tears. I glanced back at the well dressed trio who were whispering to each other and giggling as girls all over the world do when in groups. They turned and melted into the crowd.

But these women v. out
of place as they are v. smartly
and expensively dressed.

Very well dressed kids.
The girl on the left
is wearing a superb cornflower
blue tunic with a transparent
white head scarf.
Girl (?) on right wears shirt of
subtle multicoloured stripes

"Prinaka, you have given me a day which they could not. A day I will never forget. You have introduced me to your friends, you have been kind and gentle and generous. You have looked after me ... ". I did not know what to say and the gulf in joint language was too great.
"You think I kind and clever ... and pretty?"
"Yes."
"You still want to draw me?"
"Yes, of course."
"Good." The grin returned and the big almond eyes regained their sparkle.
"Rob come ... I take you home. Long way soon dark. Come."
It seemed I had been forgiven.
We had not gone very far when she stopped dead in her tracks and said:
"Oh ... sorry ... not remember tabeez shop ... we do first, OK?"
We turned back and went against the considerable flow of evening traffic eventually arriving at the shop. It was undoubtedly more up market than the street traders she had been dealing with but was still a very basic building, open to the street and protected at night by a pull down garage type door.
"I not like this man Rob. He not kind and he give me little money."
She reached round the back of her rolled up shorts ... a storage area which I had seen was considerably larger than it appeared (certain generations will remember Mother's bag in 'Swiss Family Robinson') and produced another plastic bag of tabeez.
"He always same", she explained. "Rob you maybe come with me, he married to my mother's sister and he want me do things I don't like ... maybe OK if you there?"
I looked at her quizzically but before I could ask what she meant she was round the counter holding out the small bag. The gentleman in question was, even to me, sleazy, with heavily ringed fingers and he drew on a cheap cigarette.

He treated her with an arrogant disdain unlike any of the other men we had met throughout the day. She held out the bag of tabeez at arm's length, and accepted, again at arm's length, a two taka note. He stepped closer and ran a finger across her cheek and said something. She looked at me with a mix of utter trust in her eyes and total panic in her body language.

"Rob this why I not like ... what he say what he want ... it wrong." He turned and noticed me for the first time and looked shocked that I had a note/sketch book and had obviously just taken a picture with a camera... "You know this child?" he asked with a sneer.
Suddenly everything changed ... no answer I could think of was safe to me or to Prinaka.

"I am an artist, I draw people, and my colleague here" ... gesturing towards Prinaka who was trying hard not to hide behind me "suggested I draw you"...
I handed over this sketchbook.
"Ha hoo" ... looking at Prinaka ... (and only translated by her to me) "He good ... he draw me?"
I did a sketch which he seemed to like. I tore it out of the book and gave it to him, and then we left hurriedly. He tried to delay us "Mr ... you want to buy ... I give you good price ...." brandishing some item which we did not even look at.
"Rob, I sorry ... every week he same ... horrible ... what he want, wrong, wrong ... so bad."
She spat into the gutter,
"I so hate ... I NEVER do" ... the sparkle had left her eyes again; suddenly she looked older and weary. She looked up at me the habitual grin not convincing without the twinkling eyes.
"Come Rob ...we go home."
We walked in silence for a couple of blocks before turning back into an alleyway. On the corner of the main street and the alley world was a small cafe, not much more than a couple of plastic seats and tables covered in dust on the pavement. Although it was late afternoon it was still, to me, unbearably hot.
"Can we stop for a moment Prinaka?" I asked. She did not answer but sat down on a blue chair, I sat down opposite her. Almost immediately an elderly woman with an extraordinary growth on her neck proffered a begging bowl. Before I could react Prinaka produced a few paisa and dropped them into the bowl ... I followed her example and the woman wandered on down the street.

woman begging in the street
neck v. twisted if anything
drawing understates.

"Prinaka ... I buy you a drink OK ... we sit here for a while. What would you like?"
Briefly the eyes twinkled. "Same as last time? ... No ... far too cost much. Tea ... please you."
I bought her a bottle of coke.
"In my country Prinaka, we say after something horrible has been said that it leaves a bad taste in the mouth ... this will wash the bad taste away."
"In Bengali like same ... it why I spit." She took a sip, put the bottle on the table and hunching her feet on to the seat put her arms round her legs and rested her chin on her knees. She was for a moment or two lost in her own thoughts then she looked up at me with big brown questioning eyes.
"Rob, in your country some men bad to girls?"
"Yes I am afraid so Prinaka".
"That man also boys ... he give money."
"That is horrible ... have you told anyone ... any adult?"
"You."
"You should tell your father then you would not have to go every week."
"Can't ... that man same family as my mother ... I told you ... and anyway ... many children no parent that man he do bad thing and give money ... if they get no money then not eat. I lucky my father and I work, we eat. "
She looked so fragile and vulnerable and sad. I did not know what to say and 25 years on I still do not know what I could have said or what I would say now.

We finished our drinks and set out down the alley. We had not gone very far when I became aware of a ringing bell faint in the distance. To begin with I thought it might be my hearing playing up again but, fortunately, Prinaka had heard it as well.
"Rob, you like snake?" The eyes were shining again and the grin, for the first time in a while, returned to its cheeky brilliance.
"I don't know ... you mean to eat?"
The infectious giggle had returned as well "No ... not eat ... just see ... man with snake he magicman coming ... you want see?"
A magicman with a snake was obviously something not to be missed.
"Come Rob, quick, it fun ... I know him."
We walked briskly towards the sound and eventually found at a place where two alleys crossed at right angles, a large crowd and in the centre was an extraordinary figure dressed in a white shirt and white baggy breeks with long flowing white hair, an extravagant white moustache and his white beard neatly clipped. He was an imposing figure made more so by the long snake he had draped over his shoulders. He was obviously delighted to have me in his audience because he stopped and posed with the snake for a photograph. He was performing a series of magic tricks and he was very good: a coin placed in one of the audience's top pocket reappearing in the snake's mouth, cigarettes broken in two or mashed in his fist reappearing intact in the pocket of another audience member. Every now and then he would stop and ask something and some people would come forward and whisper either in his ear or would appear to talk to the snake. He would answer and hand over a tabeez; sometimes money exchanged hands.
I asked Prinaka what he was doing and she explained that he was telling fortunes and maybe curing people.

I made a couple of quick drawings and very rapidly we became a counter amusement; indeed by the time I started on sketch number three we had the bigger audience and it seemed that the magic of drawing was winning. He was not best pleased. Prinaka found it wonderful.

The situation escalated and Mr Snakemagicman came storming towards us shouting, the big snake flapping behind him like a scarf. He seemed to be waving another smaller snake like a lasso "Come quick Rob ... he angry ... we run" ... and we did, Prinaka almost unable to because she was laughing so much. Eventually we stopped and she, still chuckling, explained that he used to buy his tabeez from her but had found a cheaper supply ... " ... very poor not nice quality like mine".

Sabotaging his sales pitch was obviously a fine bit of commercial revenge.

"My father will find very funny" she giggled.

We meandered on homeward chatting amiably; in retrospect E.H. Shepard's drawings of Winnie the Pooh and Piglet come to mind!

as drawing was a serious counter
attraction. Quite a fierce gentleman
and was not going to be persuaded

"My mother ask me to get vegetable for eat tonight ... OK to do now Rob?"
"Yes of course."
"That man there very nice he keep vegetable not so good to sell and let me have ... not many paisa ... some time no money."
She indicated a gentleman sitting behind a pile of fruit and vegetables "We wait till no one else get vegetable then go". We sat down and waited. She had lost her hair bobble in our escape from Mr Snakemagicman and her hair flopped into her eyes making her look, if anything, even younger and more vulnerable.
I produced my sketchbook and made these drawings with Prinaka watching closely.
"Rob how you learn draw?"
"I think it was something I always liked to do Prinaka, I don't think I actually learned it."
"You no teacher?"
"We did drawing and painting at school but it was not really how to draw, we learned about colours I suppose ... mixing colours ... you know blue and yellow making green, that sort of thing."
"I don't know ... how yellow and blue make green?"
I dug in my bag and found a tube of cobalt blue watercolour and another of chrome yellow ... squeezed a tiny bit of each onto my hand, spat in it and swirled the colours around.
"Your spit magic" she giggled in delight.
"No ...you try" ... I squeezed a little more on to her hand ... "Go on spit and stir." She did and chortled in delight ... "I like."
She sat drawing on the step we were sitting on with her finger, green leaf like shapes, shapes which grew eyes and then wings.
"Rob draw is my favourite bit of the world ... I love it. Here clean paper not easy and only black or blue pencil. One day maybe I book like yours ... and brush ....and colour. Rob you tell me you show me colour book?"

Man Selling bananas in Ostend

I dug the A4 watercolour sketchbook out of my bag but before I could hand it to her the fruit seller gave her a wave ... I gave her bit of cloth to wipe her hand on and she shot across the alley ... I cleaned my hands and followed her.
Ever since lunchtime when she had got me a free and very delicious lunch my conscience had been drip feeding into my thought processes. As I joined her she was bargaining furiously ... but obviously with much humour for both seller and purchaser laughed with ease throughout the transaction. Should I offer to pay? In my culture that would seem possibly rude and after the kindness she had shown me I did not want to insult or embarrass her. My eye caught a glimpse of packs of plastic hair bobbles hanging on the wall behind the fruit seller.
"OK Rob we go home now." And she set off.
I indicated to the fruit seller what I would like and he grinned and handed a pack over ... "Prinaka lost hers," he grinned ... I paid the requisite paisa ... and as I caught her up she looked at me, vaguely suspicious, head slightly to one side "What you buy?"
I handed the pack over.
Rarely has such a simple present been greeted with so much dancing delight "Rob ... thank you ... six all different colour ... I never have more than one. My mother would been very angry I lost other."
If anything, my conscience now started to work overtime; however, once a new hair bobble was in place, we continued on our way, the smaller of us once again half dancing half a step ahead.

Eventually we emerged from the gloom of an alley to find ourselves not far from a huge stadium. Many people were coming and going, preparing for nightfall. Some of the shops under the stadium were still open but most had closed and others were closing down for the night.
"We home," she announced.
I suddenly realised that from the start, from when we first met, she had said she would take me 'home' but had never asked where my hotel was so maybe this was what she thought I was looking for. I looked right and left: everything was deeply strange and new. Something like panic swept through me. I had started out lost but now I was very truly lost and it was nearly dark. I looked down at her to discover her looking at me curiously and intently judging my reaction and, inevitably, grinning.
"Prinaka this is not my hotel."
"No it is home ... my home is here. I say we go home. My father teaches me your language is good to use words for joke he call it a 'afun'."
"A pun?"
"Yes a pun ... not look worried ... I take vegetables my mother you meet my father then I take your hotel ... OK?" She was beside herself with delight at the joke!
I decided that it probably was not the best time or place to try and explain what a pun actually was and followed her.

This lad carrying water in a very
a large version of the prayer containers
mentioned earlier.

The stadium was a modern concrete affair and we walked round to what I presumed to be the back ... presumed because the lighting was not as good.
"Rob, my home."
There was a piece of blue plastic stretched between two concrete pillars to form a waterproof roof, that stretched down the back to be held in place by a piece of red carpet. A male figure was sitting working on something with his back to us and a woman, nursing a small child, was sitting stirring a pot. She looked up and her face broke into a glorious smile when she saw Prinaka. Prinaka put her finger to her lips and tip-toed up to the figure sitting with his back to us, presumably her father. She hunkered down beside him and put her arms round him. He stopped what he was doing and hugged her tightly. They talked and Prinaka handed over the days takings. She turned to me "Rob ... come ... meet my father."
I ducked down into the plastic 'tent' and he said in very good English but without turning round ... "Let me clean my hands sir, so I can shake your hand ... I understand you have been very kind and looked after my daughter today."
"I did nothing", I said, "Prinaka rescued me and has looked after me all day."
He wiped his hands on a cloth, turned round and I was faced with a man of my own age who had his daughter's warm infectious grin, and a thin moustache and beard, not unlike my own. I looked into his eyes expecting to discover where Prinaka had inherited her twinkling almond brown ones from.
He had none: only two very deep, blank, scarred, skinned-over eye sockets.
Prinaka gently placed her father's hand in mine.
"Bābā, this is Mr Rob.
Rob this is my father" ... she grinned at us both ... "Rob my father ... very wonderful ... I so love."

His hand shake was firm and the smile was very genuine and warm
"Mr Rob sir, please my name is Ayur, we would be very pleased if you would eat with us tonight."
"Ayur? Like the God?"
"Ah you recognise; that is good ... please you will join us for food?"
"Ayur I would be honoured, thank you."
"Please sit down."
"Ayur in my country it is customary for a guest to bring a gift when invited for a meal, please before I sit may I find a gift for you? I will not be long."
Prinaka was immediately concerned "Rob you get lost ... again ... I come too?"
I assured her I was not going far and walking 50 m or so around the stadium found this lad who was selling bottled drinks ... I bought four bottles of 'Sprite' and returned to Ayur's family.
"Mr Rob thank you, very nice ... I like very much and I think Prinaka never have. Please sit down."
We sat with our backs against the stadium wall, Prinaka cradling her baby sister, jammed beside her father in the corner, his arm protectively over her shoulder. Mrs Ayur (I was formally introduced but have no record of her name) cooked at the pavement edge.
Ayur told me how he had trained as an engineer and had had a good job until losing his eyes in an industrial accident shortly after meeting his wife. They, until recently, had lived in Talab, one of Dhaka's slums, but when Prinaka was old enough to trade for the family they had moved into the centre of town to give them a bigger and more easily accessed clientele. He was, he told me, saving to rent a small shop in which they could live and trade.

Once again my conscience started somersaulting.
"Mr Rob my Prinaka would very much like you to give her a drawing lesson but is too shy to ask." I looked at Prinaka and she grinned back at me. A shy Prinaka was a very new concept to me but then I suppose youngsters often behave differently when with their parents!
"Mr Ayur please tell her I would be delighted."
"Do now because after we eat it will be too dark I think. Please call me Ayur not Mr Ayur."
"Of course ... and I am just Rob."
Prinaka handed her wee sister over to her Dad and got up and squeezed in between us and the lesson commenced.
"OK Prinaka what do you want to know?" I asked.
"First see colour book please?"
I handed it over and she looked through it in silence.
"Paper ... very thick ... very nice ... I think cost many paisa? Rob you only paint things you see?"
"No at home I use the things I have in these books to try and tell stories that are in my head."
"I only draw what I see in my head ... you teach me draw what I see ... and magic colour please?"
We did a crash course in colour theory and rarely since have I had such a thrilled, excited and able student. We rapidly moved on to watercolour washes and graded washes ... "Now Rob show me how to see draw."

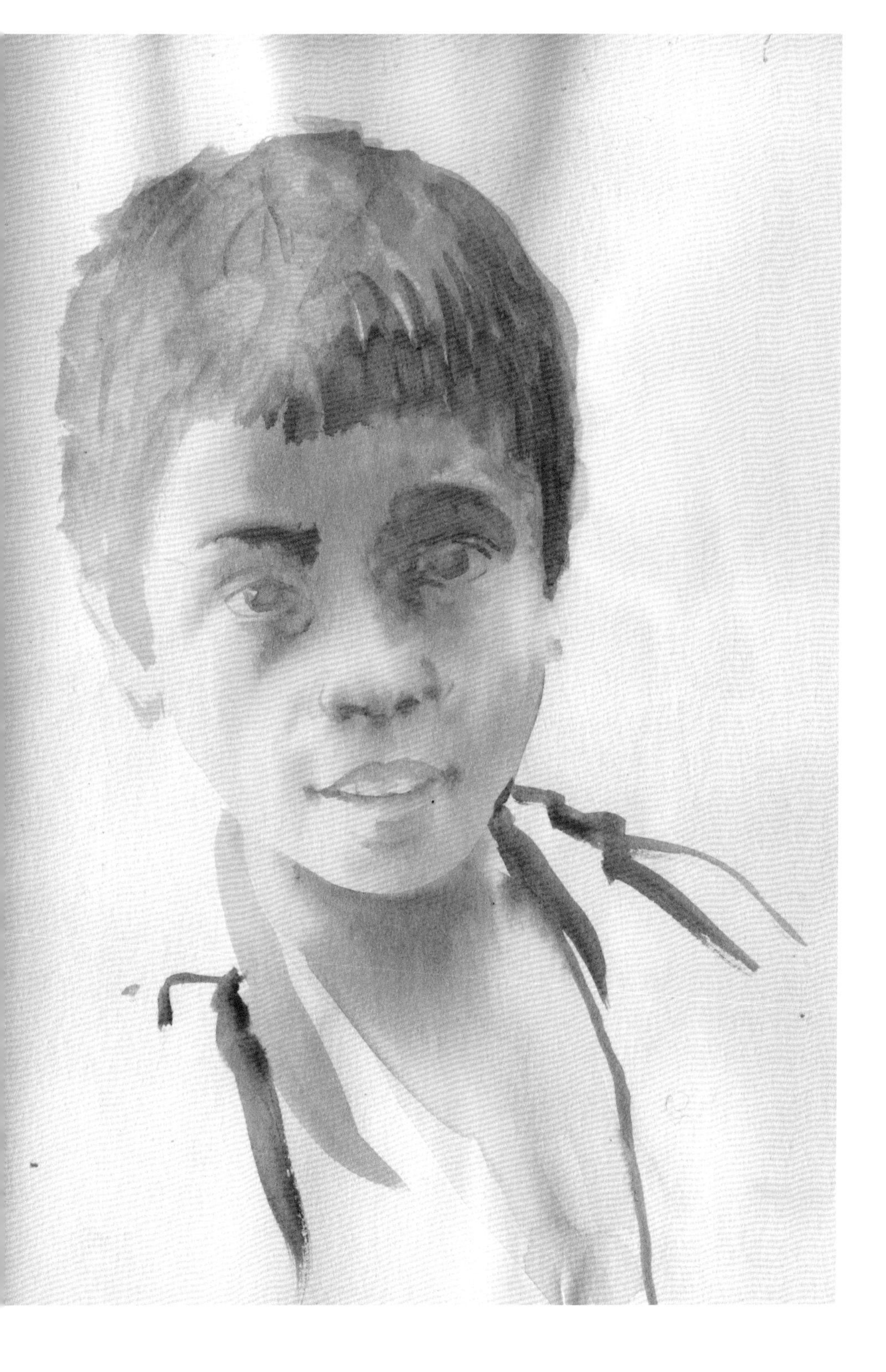

"Ah it like writing with pen at school," she stated emphatically. I looked at her curiously. "You use a pen with a bottle of ink?" I asked.
"Yes I like."
"Prinaka you are very lucky, in my country students do not get the chance any more... they used to ... but it is the best possible way of learning to draw ... with pencil or pen."
"And brush," she grinned.
I explained to her about there being no outlines in what we see and that lines that seem like outlines can end as inside a form and that you must learn to look closely "Like my mother's dress?" she asked.
I looked and saw that the folds of the dress did indeed run from the "outline" form and that if I were drawing her would undoubtedly be the main emphasis....
"I understand," she said ... "can I try?"
I handed over the sketchbook and brush.
Supper was an utterly delicious spicy fruit and vegetable curry served with rice, the bowl being placed in the centre of us and everyone helping themselves.
Ayur explained to me how he made the tiny tabeez despite having no sight: an inspired use of templates being his brilliant method. It was obvious that Ayur and his daughter were a very strong team but it seemed that ideally he really wanted her to spend more time at school.
"Ayur, I asked Prinaka how much she would sell me a tabeez for but she only said she would give me one." I said hoping I would gain an insight into what the family income was and how maybe I could help.
"Did she give you?"
"Actually no I think she forgot or sold all she had but that does not matter."

He reached in his pocket and handed me one. "A present from all of us," he said.
"Ayur, I would like to help. I would like to enable Prinaka to go to school."
"Mr Rob, you are very kind but I am an engineer and in my job I know that every bit of a machine has to be made and fitted together otherwise it will not work. If you help me then I have not made the piece, please I am not rude, but if you help maybe one day you do not, your land is a long way from here. My way is slow but I make ... I make everything myself. It is safe."
"Ayur, I respect that. You are right of course, you are a wise man. I will leave you my home address and if I can ever help please just ask. In recent years I have found myself passing through Dhaka at least twice a year ... may I bring Prinaka painting materials on my next visit?"
"Mr Rob, of course, and maybe books in English for a girl her age?"
I grinned in reply and then realised my mistake, "Yes indeed ... I will do that," I said.
(This sketch is the other one made during the art lesson to show Prinaka how to apply a wash of colour.)

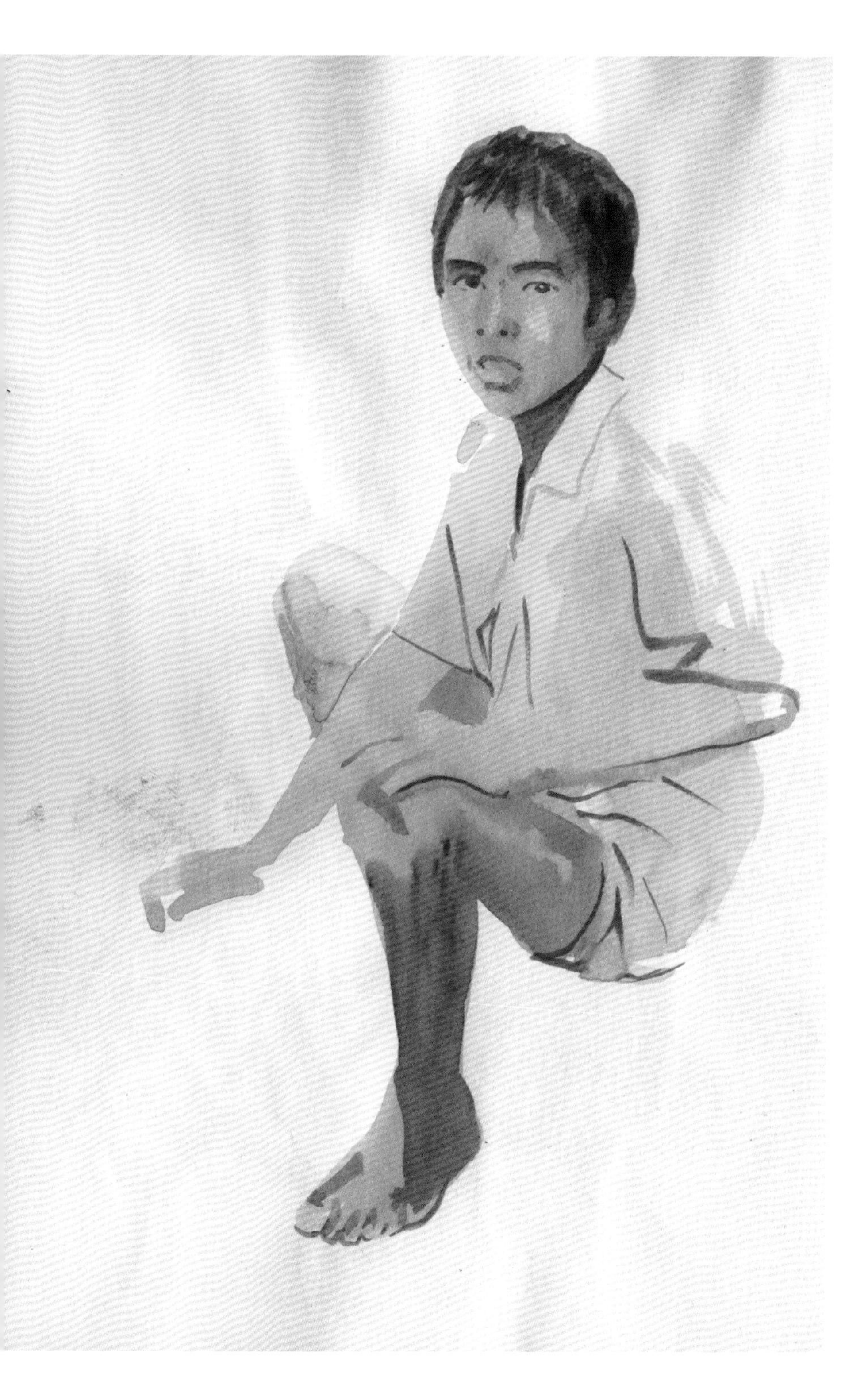

After we had eaten Ayur asked if I would like tea "Tradition in your country I think?"
"Ayur I would love tea ... "
"May I see your sketchbook?"
I handed it over and, after cleaning his fingers, he went through it gently stroking each page ... and on coming across the detail shown here said in an audible whisper ... "I think this my Prinaka?"
Prinaka was beside herself with excitement, hugging her father and obviously indicating that he was correct.
"How do you know?" I asked.
"You use thicker paint, the marks feel like the shape of Prinaka's head. Mr Rob it is very hard never to see your daughter."
I could have hugged him but, realising that this was culturally impossible, assured him that his daughter was very beautiful but, far more important, was kind and generous and fun.
"Prinaka, you show Mr Rob your drawings?"
She was suddenly embarrassed and exclaimed "B...ā...b...ā!!!"
Those of you with kids will recognise "D...A...D" or "M...U...M" always with the emphasis on the opening letter and always on a wailing dropping note rising again on the last letter ... the time worn call of the embarrassed son or daughter.
She dug under the carpet and produced what seemed to be a school maths book. Inserted between each page was her portfolio, often made of scraps of paper glued together.
Not for the first time in the day my surprise and astonishment was complete; even though I had been given a brief insight into her thought world when she sat drawing on the step of the shop with her finger, while waiting for the fruit seller.
The picture opposite was the one which I swapped for a portrait of herself.

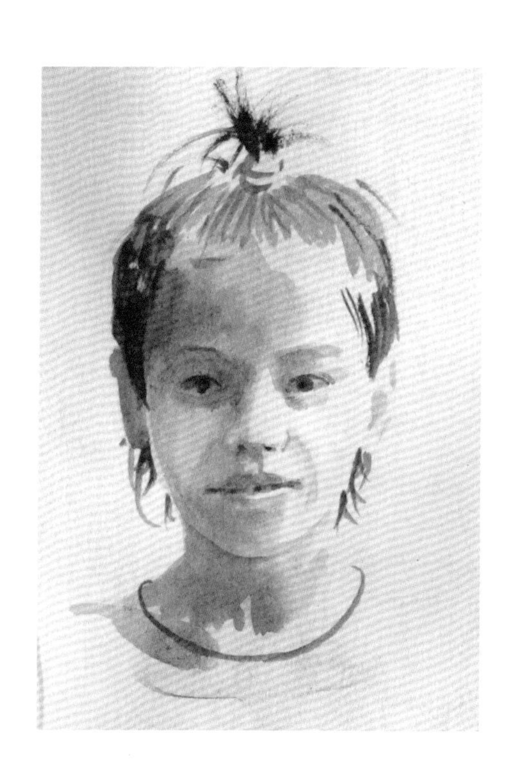

"Come Rob ... it late I take .. your hotel ... which one?"
I suddenly realised that I had not got a clue what its name was.
"Prinaka ... near a statue of birds?"
"Ah" she grinned "Balaka ... I know ... come."
I said thank you and good bye to her parents (and I did break protocol and did hug Ayur) and followed her into the dark streets. To me they were forbidding and silent, to my small guide weel kent and safe.
After about twenty minutes we emerged into a prosperous area and then suddenly into a square with, in the middle, a statue of storks. For the first time in about 12 hours I was no longer lost.
"That is my hotel Prinaka," I said, gesturing to a red coloured building on the far side.
"Good ... I go home then." She turned and was about to walk off.
"Prinaka ... come with me to the hotel please ... I have something for your father in my room. Please come."
Wary but trusting she nodded , "OK."

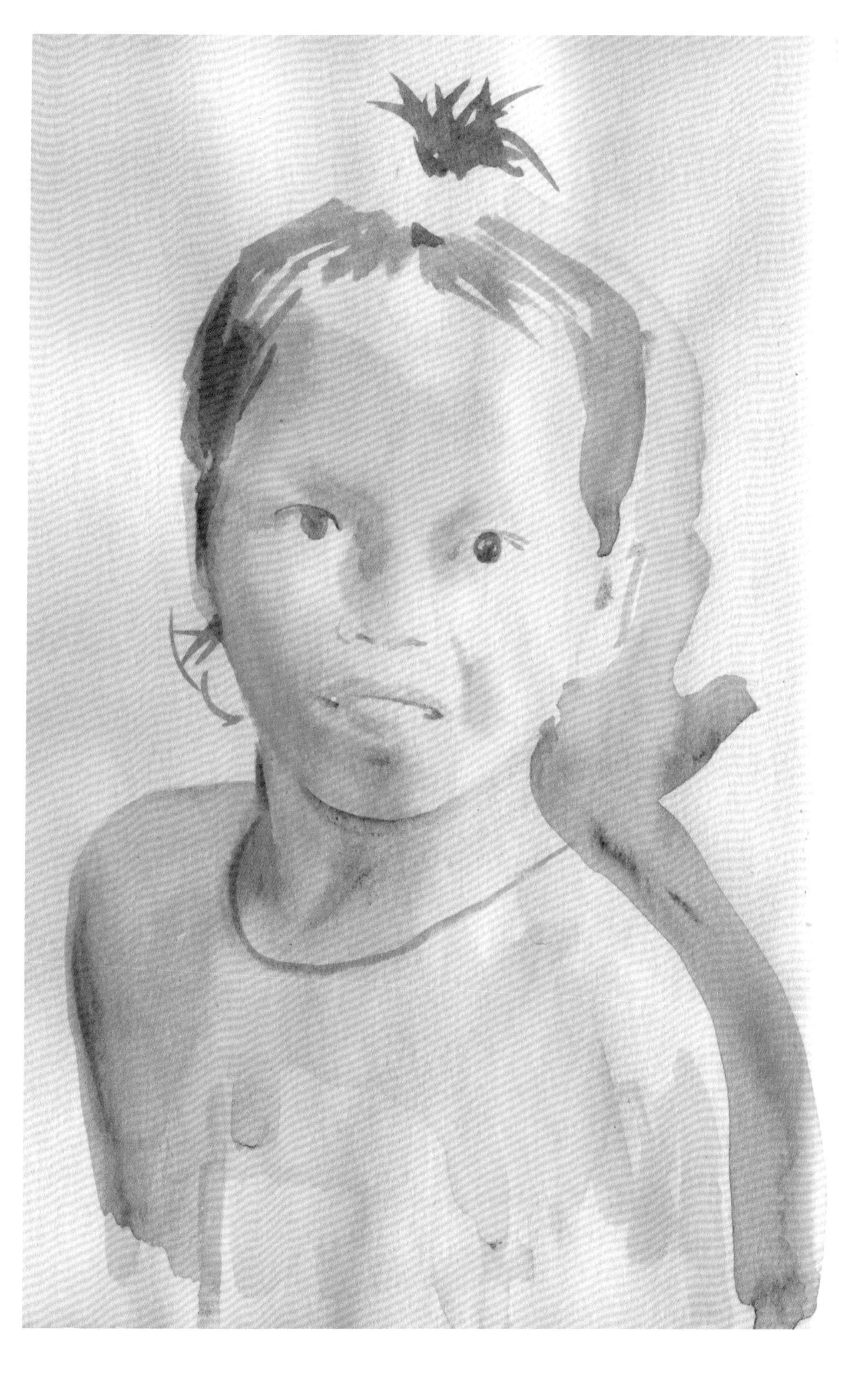

We crossed the roads and she sat on the pavements edge having refused point blank to enter the hotel lobby, as I went up to my room. Because of having to leave Nepal early I still had in my bag a brand new A4 watercolour sketchbook and an unused A5 book like the one I had been using all day. I had a couple of spare travelling brushes and a tiny set of watercolour pans in a neat plastic box (which fortuitously I had planned to give to a Nepali friend's son but because of becoming ill I had not met with) and a handful of tubes of colour ... a mixed selection of pencils and pens of various colours. I put them all in a bag. Going downstairs to reception I asked to change the last of my dollars, not much, maybe $40 or $50 perhaps a little more, into taka. I sealed an envelope with the money inside and printed on it 'Ayur ... for a rainy day'.
She was still where I had left her, a solitary figure on the side of the pavement, a child in an affluent adult world. "Give this to your father please Prinaka ... tell him it is for a rainy day. He will know what to do with it."
"Oh Rob rainy day in my country very bad ... how envelope help?"
"Your father is a clever and very wise man Prinaka ... he will make it help ... give him it please."
"OK, I do."

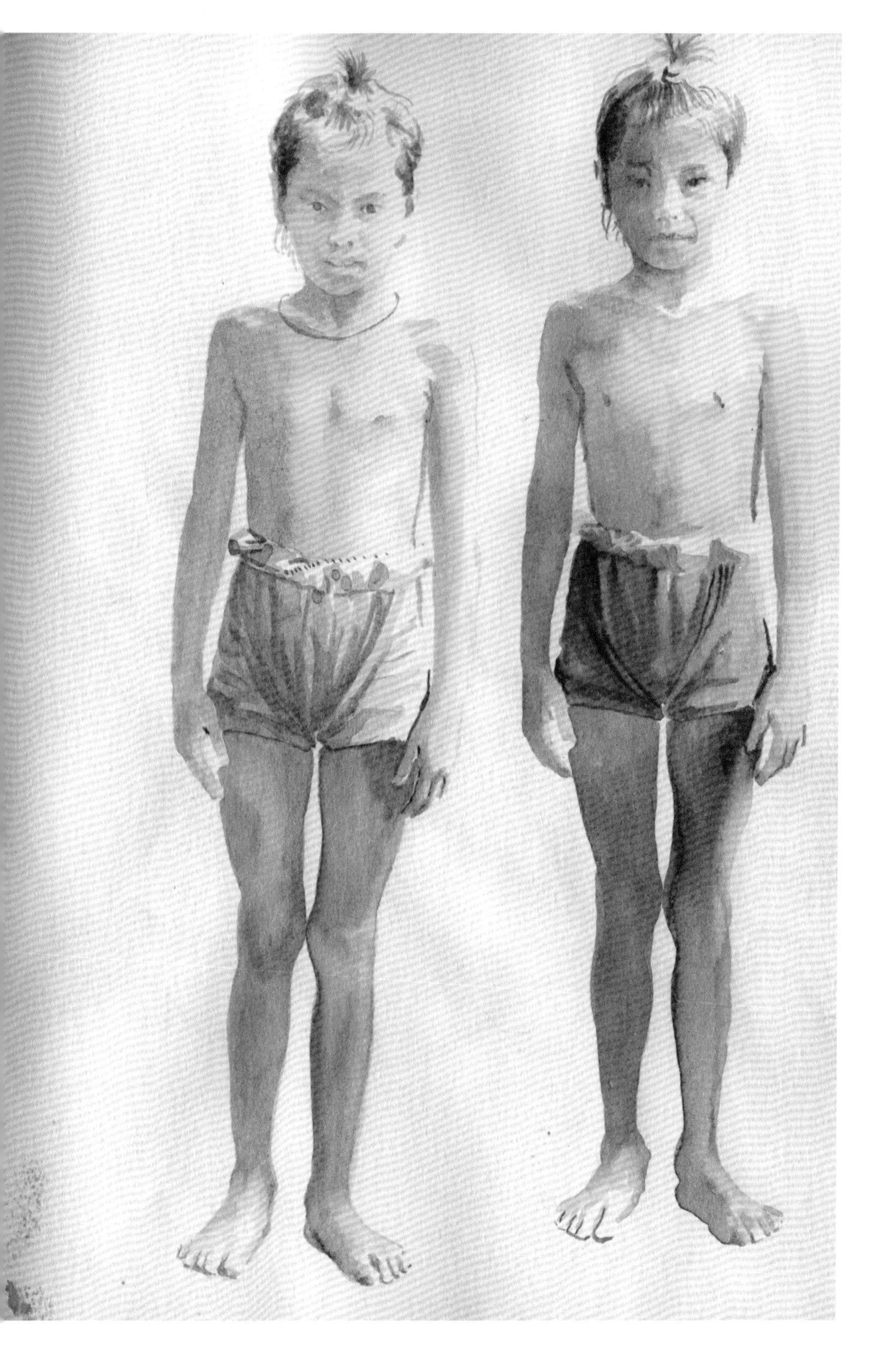

She stood up. I gave her the bag of painting equipment.
"This is for you, thank you for a most wonderful, wonderful day."
She looked inside and her eyes glittered as she looked up at me.
"Rob ... same as yours ... for me?"
I nodded.
"Day was very fun, thank you."
She turned and walked away quickly disappearing into the throngs of people still around despite the lateness of the hour.
I never saw or heard from her again.

I went back to my room in the hotel and lay on the bed thinking about the day. I do not think I slept a wink I was so much puzzled and disturbed. Eventually, around 5am, I got up and gathered my things together, checked out, and hired this lad and his beautifully decorated rickshaw to take me to the airport. Prinaka has haunted me, in the nicest possible way, almost every day since. There has hardly been a week when I have not woken around 3.30am and wondered where she is and what she is doing.

Her drawing has always had pride of place in my favourite room in my house: indeed scanning it for this has, I am sure, been the first time it has been out of its frame.

She profoundly changed me. Why did she volunteer to take me under her wing? Why, when the beggarwoman approached us, was she, who had so little, first to offer alms? All day she asked nothing from me even leaving it to her Dad to request a drawing lesson.

She changed how I understand humanity and how I understand painting and drawing.

Several months later I was appointed Highland (the part of Scotland in which I live) Council's artist-in-residence in Fort William with a remit to document the workings of the local and quite brilliant mountain rescue team. They however were in a period of transition and deep internal politics decreed that documentation would not be helpful so I was asked to work with the local primary schools instead. A bigger contrast is hard to imagine!

I wrote proper letters, these being far off pre email days, to all thirty schools but quite intentionally missing out Caol Primary which had a reputation for being hard and difficult; however I overestimated the stamps needed so by happenchance Caol became included and, I suppose inevitably, was first to respond.

There I met a couple of kids who could have been Prinaka's doubles in that they were around the same age and were fun, entrepreneurial, wondrously positive, optimistic, dangerous and worldly wise for their years. When the residency ended they (surprisingly) came up with a ploy to pay me to stay. Having learnt a huge lesson from Prinaka on the 2nd of November 1992 in Dhaka I believed in them, trusted them, and Room 13 was born.

For a few years Room 13 shook up the serious (adult) art world and those interested in arts education, with many, including Nicholas Serota, then running the Tate Galleries in London, publically stating that what the Room 13 kids were doing was the way forward. Richard Demarco called it the most important movement in Scottish Art in his lifetime. It spread worldwide but sadly, despite many attempts, never (yet) to Bangladesh.

Until this moment no one has seen the connection though I suspect my wife guessed it very quickly. But those of you who were in charge during the early Room 13 years now know why a photo of a wee Bangladeshi girl aye hung in our studio.

Room 13 still exists. Here in Scotland it is not as excitingly potent as it once was, but it thrives in a couple of schools in England (in one, the head teacher describes it as the "innovative hub" of his school), in South Africa, India, Nepal, China, Australia, Spain, Turkey, France and the USA. ...
Prinaka's legacy lives on.

I hope she does.

Rob Fairley

Rob Fairley was born in 1953 and educated at Edinburgh College of Art. After college he moved to the Scottish west coast port of Mallaig. This he 'shared' with the American painter Jon Schueler though the younger man never found the courage to knock on the seniors door. A fact he now deeply regrets!

He moved from Mallaig to the island of Shona Beag in 1975, where he lived what has been described as an 'hermetic' existence, living as much as possible off the land and from the sea and making ephemeral land based work. This work recorded, for the most part, in pinhole camera images (the camera often being made from animal carcases) was not exhibited until 2011 when the Resipole Gallery mounted a retrospective of his 'Early Work.'

All his work is based on the land and although very often it is not topographical it always relates in some way to the landscape and the weather, geology, stories, traditions, songs, myths that this encompasses and what has been called the 'terra incognito' of the human mind' that is influenced by it.

Portrait of Rob Fairley by Vadim Levin

One man exhibitions

Resipole Studios	Ardnamurchan 2019
Open Eye Gallery	Edinburgh 2012
Resipole Studios	Ardnamurchan 2011
Room 13 Gallery	Fort William 1999
Open Eye Gallery	Edinburgh 1999
Meghraj Gallery	London 1998
Open Eye Gallery	Edinburgh 1996
West Highland Museum	Fort William 1995
Open Eye Gallery	Edinburgh 1993
Open Eye Gallery	Edinburgh 1991
Open Eye Gallery	Edinburgh 1989
Inverness Museum and Art Gallery	Inverness 1986
Open Eye Gallery	Edinburgh 1986
Inverness Museum and Art Gallery	Inverness 1984
Open Eye Gallery	Edinburgh Festival 1984
Open Eye Gallery	Edinburgh 1982
Inverness Museum and Art Gallery	Inverness 1981
Henderson Gallery	Edinburgh 1979
St Stephen Gallery	Edinburgh Festival 1977
Saltire Society	Edinburgh 1976
Undercroft Gallery	Edinburgh Festival 1975

Selected group shows

ECA 75	Edinburgh 2019
Uneducated	Melbourne 2014
The Painted Lady	Edinburgh 2009
Indo/British Group 2	Mumbai,Delhi,Kolkata 2005
Indo/British Group	Mumbai, Delhi, Kolkata 2002/03
New Aspects of Painting	Gallery 54, New Delhi 2000
Five Scottish Painters	Sutton Coldfield 2001
Room 13 retrospective	Inverness and Fort William museums 2001
Young Contemporaries	Kathmandu 2000/2001
Indo/British Group	Kolkata 2000
Scottish Landscape Painting	CPS 1999/2000
Rob Fairley & Wendy Sutherland	WHM. Fort William. 2000
Five contemporary artists	Gallery 54, New Delhi 1999
The Need to Draw	Open Eye Gallery, Edinburgh 1999
Indo/British Group	Meghraj Gallery, London 1997
The Mountain Experience	Highland Regional Council 1991/2
Highland Open	1988/90/92
Scottish Art, Two Generations	City Art Centre, Edinburgh, 1982
Paisley Art Institute	1982

Scottish Contemporary Painting	Edinburgh 1979
Cleveland Drawing Biennale	1979
Scottish Tourist Board,	Birmingham 1975
Pernod Competition	Edinburgh 1975

Collections

Dundee University Archive 2011/438, 440, 448, 464, 472
George Watson's College
Glasgow Chamber of Commerce
Hamilton Education Department
Highland Regional Council
Inverness Museum and Art Gallery
Leysin University
Marine Harvest
Meghraj Collection
National Irish Visual Arts Library (NIVAL) correspondence between Rob Fairley and Peter Haining
National Library of Scotland ("An Olympus in the Dream" HB6.215.4.9 and HB6.215.3.58)
National Library of Scotland (sketchbooks and correspondence between Rob Fairley and Marshall Anderson HP4.95.1245 (Acc.13227))
Scottish Sports Council
Strathclyde Regional Council
West Highland Museum
Young Artists Group Kathmandu
And in private collections in Australia, Bangladesh, Canada, England, France, Germany, Holland, Hungary, India, Ireland, Italy, Nepal, Japan, Scotland, South Africa, Switzerland, the USA and Wales

Author of

'Jemima, the paintings and memoirs of Jemima Blackburn'
Published by, Canongate 1988. ISBN 0-86241-186-6

Blackburn's Birds'
Published by, Canongate 1991. ISBN 0-86241-436-9

'Drawing Hands and Feet'
Published by , David and Charles 2001. ISBN 0-7153-1022-4

Room 13' Social and Critical Practices in Art Education
Edited by Dennis Atkinson and Paul Dash
Published by Trentham 2005. ISBN – 13 978-185856-311-4